PROJECT

OJECT

ECONOMICS: THIS THING THEY CALL GROWTH IS A FALLACY

Beginning with the minimum wage law in 1938 using the term growth is one of the biggest lies in economics that have ever been told. Sure, in a true free market place economy like before the 1938 minimum wage law the term growth meant real true growth.

That is simply because it is impossible to have consumer inflation and a welfare state absent a minimum wage law. But, after the liberals enacted the 1938 minimum wage law what is now called growth is some kind of a phony blend of mostly inflation with hardly any real growth to speak of. And it's been that way ever since 1938. Today it takes $50.00 or more to buy what $5.00 would eighty years ago.

Ain't no sense of me rambling on and on, I'll just get to the point one way or another our insane arch-evil 1938 socialist minimum wage law must go. If we don't do it ourselves soon mother natures supreme law of "Natural Selection" is going to do it for us. And that means totally collapsing the economy, period.

I have been yelling out a primal survival stress call for many years now, what else is there to be done? Untold millions are going to starve to death. We have very little foundation like a strong nuclear and extended family system and an adequate supply of small farmers and home gardeners for emergency bartering capacity left to rebuild upon.

A total USA economy collapse may set modern civilization back to the Stone Age, for real.
SIRMANS LOG: 28 AUGUST 2016, 2209 HOURS.

OUR WELFARE ANNIVERSARY

Because of its twenty-year anniversary I see the welfare debate is being tossed around. The blessing I have is I have the perspective and depth to see pass fog and bull and bore right to the heart of most problems. The first thing is if you don't understand human survival everything you say is empty rhetoric anyway.

Anyone that has any knowledge of history should know that across all cultures one thing has been a constant for human survival for over six thousand years. This thing has proven itself to sustained life and has withstood the test of time. If you don't know what I'm talking about by now you don't have a true sense of history or what it takes for human survival, period.

This thing I'm talking about is the "Nuclear and extended family system". There has never been a society in the history of mankind across all cultures that survived without a strong "Nuclear and extended family system" in place, period. Yet, the USA and Western Europe with their welfare states has left the traditional strong "Nuclear and extended family system" in almost total ruins.

With that being the case hardly anyone is making sure proper norms and traditions is instilled in the very young. In far too many cases a strong male disciplinarian head of household is nowhere to be found. And even if a male is in the picture he is there for stud service at her whim.

It is a waste of time talking about reforming welfare because it is just one more monster in our liberalism swamp. I can see right to the core of our welfare problem, and tell you the way to solve it. The best way is to kill two birds with one stone by starving the beast and draining the swamp. It is very simple; just repeal the arch-evil 1938 socialist minimum wage law, period.

That act would starve the liberalism beast to death and drain the liberalism swamp all at the same time. If that happened it would also untie the USA economy and give it back its disciplining power and bring on a booming economy all at the same time. Otherwise, it will be impossible for the USA economy not to totally collapse soon.

Don't take my word, any USA economist in private will tell you the same thing if he/she trust you.
SIRMANS LOG: 21 AUGUST 2016, 1332 HOURS.

USA ECONOMICALLY INSANE ARCH-EVIL 1938 SOCIALIST MINIMUM WAGE LAW:
Enough is enough, if congress is not going to repeal this evil 1938 law, me or someone must contest this evil law in court to the highest level, period. The 10th amendment is there for a reason; each state should have the power to set its own minimum wage law or if to set one at all.

A minimum wage law gives the government total power over all property rights, all production rights, and all distribution rights. There is no greater governmental power on earth than to have a minimum wage law. Plus, it turns a free market place into a p.... economy with no power to discipline itself or to protect the country's culture and morals.

It is impossible to save the USA unless our evil 1938 minimum wage law is repealed. Only a genuine true free market place economy can save the USA from the liberals and total doom, period. And that can never happen with a minimum wage law in place.
SIRMANS LOG: 19 AUGUST 2016, 1129 HOURS.

AUTHORITARIAN RULE IS INEVITABLE IF THE LIBERALS WIN THE NOVEMBER 2016 PRESIDENTIAL ELECTION

One thing I have learned is individual freedom cannot exist very long without a non minimum wage genuine true free market place economy in place to maintain societal discipline, period. I hate to admit it but I believe after our November 2016 presidential election individual freedom in the USA will be lost forever.

If the liberals win they will take over the U.S. Supreme Court. If that happens there will be no saving individual freedom, liberalism will have the final say on everything. It shouldn't take a rocket scientist to know that mass civil unrest will only be a matter of time and then authoritarian rule will become inevitable. God save the USA.

NOTE CONCERNING TRUMP:

The way this writer see it is when you have a corrupt anti-survival hostile liberal news media hell bent on destroying you: Damn the torpedoes! Full speed ahead!

An aggressive, persistent, and determine person can never be counted out; unforeseen forces tends to come to the aid of someone like that.

The last three republican presidential losers let the anti-survival corrupt liberal news media steam roll over them without even breaking a sweat. Not so with Trump, at least he will take them to the mat.
SIRMANS LOG: 13 AUGUST 2016, 0917 HOURS.

TRUMP, THE LIBERALS NEMESIS

Always remember that Mother Nature leans toward creating and maintaining a balance in the universe. So, maybe that could be the role of Trump in the grand scheme of things.

Something definitely needs to bring some balance to the totally out of control liberalism in the USA and Western Europe, period. Liberalism is a do-good weak shallow minded way of thinking in this writers view.

But, the world would be a very dark dreary place to live without liberalism; it is the spice of life when kept in balance. However, with few exceptions they just don't have the depth to make the best leaders.

Liberals will give away the store to grab and hold on power, especially if it's not their own to give away in the first place. Never in history has the poor ever been liberal until the welfare state came along and destroyed accountability and responsibility.

I will explain liberalism in four words: "Lack of survival awareness".
SIRMANS LOG: 12 AUGUST 2016, 1025 HOURS.

TRUMP VERSUS THE LIBERALISM FRENZY
Most liberals can't recognize or take a joke. I've said this many times and will say it again; liberals have a problem separating the real from the unreal, period. The fact is people with sound judgment and common sense doesn't have a big problem with Trump. Sure, common sense people disagree strongly with him, but they will never go into a frenzy.

Trump sends liberals into a frenzy where they think Trump is in fantasy land when it is liberalism itself that is a fantasy land swamp. And for the umpteenth time I repeat that the only thing that can rein in liberalism and force it back under control is repealing our 1938 minimum wage law, period.

Otherwise, nothing can stop liberals and liberalism from totally destroying this last bastion of individual freedom left in the world today. I write it as I see it, period. Most people know what happens when you dingle a cross in front of a vampire, well, Trump has a similar affect on most liberals. Now, only a fool or liberal would take what I just said as a fact of life.

People are beginning to see liberalism as out of control in the USA. And I will go, as far as to say out of control liberalism is a greater threat to USA survival than anything I can imagine and I mean that literally. It must be brought under control if the USA has any chance of survival, and only repealing the 1938 minimum wage law can bridle liberalism, period.

I have but one vote, which I will never use to aid a liberal take over of the U.S. Supreme Court. That is the USA number one problem now; liberalism has taken over damn near everything else already. And if they finally get control of the U.S. Supreme Court it will definitely be all over in terms of us being a free people and nation.

SIRMANS LOG: 09 AUGUST 2016, 2316 HOURS.

WHO GAVE THE LIBERAL NEWS MEDIA THE RIGHT TO PLAY GOD?

Talking about scary and the nuclear button: I think what is far more scarier is the maximum volume of emotionalism that is being spewed out by the shallow minded liberal news media. This today's corrupt liberal news media is an insane mad-house of muck, negativism, and partisanship far above reason.

It is like a tree-top wild fire, practically no one can stand up against it and survive, and especially those in politics. It scares me almost to death for my beloved country, sound judgment and common sense be damned. We have a down-right out of control anti-survival propaganda machine loose upon the land in my view.

About this Trump thing: Whatever happened to allowing the voters to make up their own minds? What give the liberal news media the right to play God and demand for the people what is political correct for the survival of this great nation?

Far too many republicans just don't get it, it is not just Trump, any republican nominee is going to be ripped apart by this anti-survival liberal news media propaganda machine even if they have to invent a reason, it is sheer madness.

Don't insult my intelligence, I know right from wrong and my conscience will punish me if I knowingly do wrong. Since the come about of our liberal induced welfare state far too many people has a weak to no conscience at all.

A strong conscience is something that has to be instilled when very young by means of a reward or punishment method. Love and praise acts as a reward whereas criticism and rejection acts as punishment to a child. But, when not abused, nothing instills a more strong and powerful conscience in a child than corporal punishment.

"Spare the rod you spoil the child" is why we have so much more crime today than any time in history.
SIRMANS LOG: 03 AUGUST 2016, 1202 HOURS.

LIBERALS ARE MASTERS AT THE TRIPLE OPTION USING MISDIRECTION AND HIDING THE BALL
I can't speak for anyone else, but as for me I'm not going to lose sight of the ball, ever. In my view the ball

is the U.S. Supreme Court. If the liberals succeed in hiding the ball and capture the U.S. supreme court its over folks there will be no recovery for the USA, period. I'm a firm believer that there is no greater noble deed than helping the poor, disadvantage, and the needy.

However, that is something that must be done by the private sector and never by government except as a last resort on a set temporary basis only. The reason is when government sets out to help the poor, disadvantage, and the needy it destroys the nuclear and extended family system and eventually the whole country, for real.

Right now in the USA I would estimate around 99 percent of the people think I'm wrong on this but I'm not. And that is proof why we are doomed as a free people and a free nation. Only repealing the 1938 minimum wage law can save the USA. In terms of human survival when you destroy the nuclear and extended family system there is no foundation left to rebuild upon, it is over in terms of human survival.

In history there has never been a society that survived without a healthy nuclear and extended family system, period. Our liberal induced welfare state has destroyed our USA nuclear and extended family system to the point of almost total ruins. God save us. "The truth will set you free".

WAKE UP PEOPLE:
Sometimes a nation has to learn the hard way there are no free rides in nature, everything has a price. Ignoring that fact the liberals has spendthrift this great nation to its knees up to 20,000,000,000,000 in debt. Now, one way or another we all are going to pay dearly in blood, sweat, and tears.

All government wealth originates from some form of private business profit and even if government taxed 100 percent it couldn't support our current welfare state. It is simply impossible for the USA economy not to collapse from its social and family provider burdens at some point soon.

Repealing the 1938 minimum wage law will slowly wean government out of the social and family provider business, otherwise we can kiss individual freedom goodbye forever. And who knows where it all ends. Lord have mercy.
SIRMANS LOG: 27 JULY 2016, 0007 HOURS.

THE AWESOME HEALING POWER OF LOVE AND FORGIVENESS

There is an age old saying: "To be a good leader you first must be a good follower". I find that to be as true today as ever. To a great extent today's mentality tends to be: Me first, I want mine, I want it all, screw you, and self-sacrifice and putting God and country above all else be damned.

As for me, I'm not going to let anyone turn me into a petty, bitter, hateful, angry, and unforgiving person, because that is a sure path that leads to self-destruction. God save the USA.
SIRMANS LOG: 21 JULY 2016, 1246 HOURS.

PS: The thing that is going to defeat Trump is he is perceived as being unable to forgive. And the only thing that can counter that belief is for him to start stressing and speaking about the power of forgiveness, or even turn to a minister for support on this. Otherwise, from fear not enough voters will ever trust him with the nuclear button.

This constant drum beat propaganda of being unfit is

designed to create doubt and fear in the voters and it definitely seems to be working.

GREAT WRITER, FREDDIE LEE SIRMANS, SR. SHARES HIS STRUGGLES

Sure, I'm neurotic and not normal and never will be. But, one thing I'm not and never will be is a loser. All of my life I have been counted out and sometimes ridiculed, laughed at, and told as a very young child that I would never amount to anything. Yet, today as a seventy three year old I am still plodding along like a zombie trying in my own way to do good and make this a better world.

I'm not educated, I have never took a computer course in my life and have never read Adam Smith or any of the great economic thinkers. But, I understand and can dissect an economy as well as anyone. So, when I tell you our insane Arch-evil 1938 socialist minimum wage law must be repealed to save the USA and western civilization, You had better believe it, period. **SIRMANS LOG: 19 JULY 2016, 2256 HOURS.**

COP KILLING GALORE! OMG!

Liberalism gone amuck is why our societal discipline has gone to hell in the USA. Only a genuine true free market place economy has the discipline and power to save the USA and western civilization from total self-destruction.

The only workable solution is obvious, the insane arch-evil 1938 socialist minimum wages law must be repealed to free and untie our USA economy before it is too late. Without a doubt I am right on this even if this supernatural wisdom is never heeded. Glory be to God.
SIRMANS LOG: 17 JULY 2016, 2257 HOURS.

RELIGION TURNOUT WILL DECIDE NOVEMBER 2016 PRESIDENTIAL ELECTION

The religious people are all in and totally committed to pushing back on all of this mass culture rot and moral decay that is taking down this great land of the free and home of the brave.

They know this is the last chance to save the USA from mass same sex marriages, the morning after pill, and mass killing on demand in the womb. Even an idiot should know that our future survival as a nation is in grave danger.

The religious people they all will be turning out in droves in November 2016 to put a stop to this insane madness that is determined to make us all amoral misfits. However, today most low-income voters don't give a damn about good morals unless it pleases their own personal biases.

We all should be praying for our future because a totally economic collapse is going to soon hit causing millions upon millions to starve to death. Of course I pray something like this will never happen, but anyone that thinks it can't ever happen is a fool.

Our nuclear and extended family system is in almost total ruins. Plus, with our mass culture rot and moral decay we now have practically no foundation left to rebuild upon, period. When I yell, scream, jump up and down, and even cry to repeal our insane arch-evil 1938 socialist minimum wage law that is a primal last chance stress call for the survival of my beloved homeland. Glory be to God.

When will men/women of common sense and sound judgment finally realize that the days of a welfare state is over, I guess circumstance will just have to show them the hard way.

SIRMANS LOG: 12 JULY 2016, 1120 HOURS.

PS: I believe it will be a lot less likely that Trump will get impeached if Newt is selected for vice president??? The liberal lawmakers are already 100 percent for it, then sprinkle in a few republicans and it will be done.

RACISM! SO, WHAT ABOUT IT?

There are some subjects I tend to avoid and stay away from and "Racism" is one of them. I'm not good at pulling punches and I believe in calling a spade a spade, period. I view character and showing respect far more important than whether one may or may not be a racist, besides who really knows what someone is hiding deep down in his/her heart anyway. Someone laughing in your face may be the biggest racist of all.

If one has a secure and independent mindset who gives a damn what someone else may or may not think as long as they can't hurt you. As long as there are different races racism is going to exist in some form to some degree, period. The real problem and threat as far as I'm concern is bigotry when race is used to punish or hurt another race.

I think the real problem with my race, which is the African American race, is we have not shedded our dependency slave mentality. Sure, it kept us alive during and right after slavery in a totally hostile environment, but now we are responsible for our own survival as a race and as individuals. We act like the white man the government or someone else is responsible for our personal survival.

From a mentality point of view I think we view other blacks like inferior competing siblings instead of independent adults that need to help and support each other. In my view that is the reason behind all of this mass senseless violence in black communities.

We don't see other African Americans as lovable and needed racial family members like before the "New Deal". But, instead see an inferior rival threat undeserving of respect. Boom. Before the "New Deal" blacks were forced to need and support each other, and black culture and enterprise thrived far, far more than today.

Also, blacks were beginning to shed its dependency slave mentality and bam; the "New Deal" booted the black male disciplinarian out of the house. I've said enough and will close by saying this: As long as our welfare state last African Americans will be voting 90 percent plus Democrat until dooms day, it is because of an unneeded crutch in my view.

RAW! CRUDE! MIND BOGGLING! THE REAL TRUTH ABOUT THE BLACK PSYCHE IN AMERICA
The betterment of a race or people must be pulled up from the top by its elites because only they have the resources. But, because of Du Bois's victory over the minds of black Americans the black elites has left black communities in almost total ruins in my view.

I believe only blacks can save their own communities, no other race or people is going to do it, period. At the time many decades ago Booker T lost the battle for the minds of black people to Du Bois. Well, I'm one that believes that Booker T may have lost the battle but he never lost the war and I'm living proof of that fact.

Booker T believed that blacks should strive to be self-sufficient, whereas Du Bois believed that blacks should focus on the best education to be successful and accepted by the larger society. So, here we are today many decades later with most black leadership and black elites having abandoned, deserted, and living as for away from a black community as they can afford.

Except for Funeral homes, old churches and maybe a few barber shops and beauty parlors just about every other black elite business has hauled ass out of black communities. The problem is before one can have a free and independent mentality one first must want to strive to be self-sufficient at all cost.

I believe Blacks today are still following the Du Bois formula of wanting to be loved and accepted by others to prove ones worth. A self-sufficient people don't have a need to prove their worth. They already have respect for themselves and know how to show respect for other people, too.

What kind of a people will vote 90 percent plus for one political party for 50 years and still be on their knees hat in hand. I'm just one lonely neurotic writer with my own opinion; thank God I can still share it without disappearing in the middle of the night.

There are no Juke joints and chitlin circuits anymore. There are no thriving exciting black enterprise zones anymore. In my young days there were many clubs, lounges, and places to go including places for teens to dance and have fun, too. But, back then teens knew how to behave, which they don't today and is the reason very few will provide teen centers anymore.

I remember so well when I was a teenager they had a soda shop in my hometown where teens could hangout and dance. Back then a little bit of money would buy a lot. You could get a foot long slaw dog for 25 cent plus a penny tax. A many of time I would get me a slaw dog and be good to go and just hangout and enjoy myself.

However, with our liberal induced welfare state black culture has almost totally been destroyed. Sad, sad, but be aware the destruction of the black culture is like the canary in the mine.
SIRMANS LOG: 10 JULY 2016, 1532 HOURS.

THE MASS KILLING OF SLAVE BLOOD YOUNG BLACK MALES

Let me say up front I would never be a lawman; it's not for me. Also, I should never be writing an article on this subject because I may step on too many toes. But, knowing me I will proceed. First, I believe an economic collapse or rebirth will soon happen in the USA and all of western civilization. The USA and Western Europe and their welfare state's all are too deep and lost in mass liberalism swamps, period.

In the USA what started our whole culture and financial destruction and decline was the enacting of the 1938 minimum wage law. Enacting that law allowed the liberals to grab and hold power by inflating the dollar, which started our welfare state. Without a minimum wage law the dollar cannot be inflated, period. That said, now lets get down to why so many slave blood young blacks are being killed.

The two main reasons are a lack of respect for authority and very little self-restraint due mainly to no strong male disciplinarian in the home. However, there are several other lesser factors at play. One of the biggest lesser factors at play is young black males are stereotyped as being aggressive and violent. And that in itself causes a certain amount fear in a lot of people.

Stereotyping is unfair and not a good thing but there is

always some truth in every stereotype. Plus, there is also a racial element involved, a white victim can ask why, and all kinds of questions and get away with it whereas blacks seldom can in my view. One can be as docile as a lamb, still occasionally a cop may be abusive but that is the rare exception in my view.

Almost all cops will show restraint if one doesn't show rebellion and aggression. Here is some common sense rules if stopped by law enforcement: Keep both hands on the top of the steering wheel, if told to get on the ground you get on the ground, and above all don't make any fast or sudden moves especially in this day and time. Remember, this is an extremely dangerous time for anyone that wares a badge, and we must have order and some one have to enforce it.

I'm going to do a little ranting:
I believe the biggest failure in the black communities is black leaders and elites. They could establish high pecking order zones near black communities instead of getting as far as they can afford from an all or nearly all black neighborhood. I believe the elites are running away from themselves by deserting and not truly loving and accepting a black identity, just thinking out loud y'all.

I think so called black leadership ought to be trying to get more jobs and promoting positive values themselves in black communities instead of expecting the government and the white man to do all of the providing. Respect begets respect.

THE RAW POWER OF THE USA LIBERAL NEWS MEDIA NOISE MACHINE
There is an old saying that "Beauty is in the eyes of the beholder". Well, our liberal news media noise machine see racism and negativity hiding behind every

tree. Positive successful well-meaning people never dwell on the negative; they address the negative and move on. Only shallow small-minded haters dwell on the negative.

I believe our negative liberal news media noise machine is the biggest anti-survival monster in our USA welfare state liberalism swamp. Only repealing our God forsaken insane arch-evil 1938 socialist minimum wage law has the power to drain this swamp.

I believe the November 2016 election only determines our speed toward total doom; only repealing above said law will rein in liberalism's death march toward total doom. Of course 98 percent of the USA population think I'm a fool, nut case, idiot, and don't know what the hell I'm talking about because they can't see what I can see with my great almost supernatural wisdom.

I can't convince anyone of anything, I'm just trying to do God will and fulfill my destiny, glory be to God.
SIRMANS LOG: 05 JULY 2016, 1349 HOURS.

A MUSLIM WORLD FACT BY A GREAT WRITER
I have said it before and will say it again. In my view the biggest problem in the Muslim world is western influence and meddling. Modern western liberalism has all but totally destroyed their traditional strongman system that kept peace for centuries.

The west is determined to make its weak morally challenged welfare state democracies one size fits all replace what has worked for fifteen centuries; it is totally insane in my view, period.
SIRMANS LOG: 03 JULY 2016, 1018 HOURS.

NO SENSE OF HUMOR:
Mexican plane above, it's getting ready to attack, that's dry humor for Christ sake! Screw you if you can't take a joke is my view. Too many liberals have a problem with separating the real from the unreal. Humor is the spice of life, don't be a sourpuss. Hell, you can barely get a comedian to perform on a collage campus anymore because of liberalism and extreme political correctness.
SIRMANS LOG: 01 JULY 2016, 0841 HOURS.

ABORTION ON DEMAND IS STUPID AND MADNESS.
Procreation and future USA human survival is now under siege. Abortion on demand is flat-out murder and pain in the womb in my view. If no one protects the unborn while we have mass gay marriages, the morning after pill, porn galore, and contraceptives to no end, then where will future human being come from?

Without the repeal of our God forsaken arch-evil 1938 socialist minimum wage law there is no future USA survival in my view. The USA is far too deep and lost in our liberalism swamp and only repealing the insane God forsaken arch-evil 1938 socialist minimum wage law will drain this swamp, period. England seems to be finding it way out of their liberalism swamp.
SIRMANS LOG: 28 JUNE 2016, 1043 HOURS.

I WILL NEVER JOIN A BANDWAGON AND PUNK-OUT TO LIBERALISM
Like a broken record, play it again Sam. No minimum wage laws no immigration problems. It doesn't get any simpler than that. No getting rid of minimum wage laws soon no western civilization.

I will go as far as to say the come about of minimum wage laws is the single most cause for the decline and destruction of western civilization, period.

Everybody is thinking that the worst problems for the USA and Western Europe are immigration and finance. However, I beg the difference, I think the gravest problem for the west is culture. Too few teach the young proper norms and traditions due to our welfare states. Also, I think we are now entering an era where my books and writing may become respected.

USA 1938 socialist minimum wage law must be repealed soon or we face total civil disorder and doom, period. The law must be respected. We are a nation that is supposed to be ruled by law not by emotions and sensationalism.

To most liberals at heart gun control means taking all guns out of the hands of law abiding citizens as their final goal. They plan to do it small baloney slice by slice until it is finally achieved.

My word may not be worth much, but personally I would rather see a candidate lose fighting for the survival of my country than to join a bandwagon and punk-out to liberalism sure doom. Duh, we'll see.

The fatal mistake the last three republican presidential losers made was trying to be an appeaser to everyone and being all over the map. It takes a pit bull like bite down on two or three great issues and never letting up. Otherwise, the all powerful negative liberal news media soap opera like noise machine will drown out any hope of getting any positive message through.

All of this liberal news media talk of being helpful to any republican is disingenuous at best, they want you to lose, lose, and lose.

SIRMANS LOG: 20 JUNE 2016, 2038 HOURS.

I'M SEEING PARTISAN ATTACK DOG LIBERAL PROPAGANDA PARADING AS NEWS, WHEN WILL THE REAL NEWS PEOPLE CARE ABOUT THEIR PROFESSION. IT IS ALREADY ALONG WITH USE CAR SALESMEN.

INSTEAD OF PEOPLE ON TV TRYING TO OBJECTIVELY REPORT THE NEWS AS IS, FAR TOO MANY ARE MAKING, SHAPING, AND DISTORTING THE NEWS TO FIT THERE OWN SUBJECTIVE LIBERAL AGENDA.

HYSTERIA AND MUCK RAKING RULES THE DAY, USA FREE PRESS HAS BEEN TAKEN OVER BY EXTREME LIBERALISM, USA, USA, USA...

IS THE DEMOCRATIC PARTY AND LIBERAL NEWS MEDIA ONE AND THE SAME?
I got news for any republican or conservative that thinks another candidate would fare better with the liberal news media, then you are deluding yourself. I believe the liberal news media and the Democratic Party is one and the same, period.

No one is perfect, but at least "The Donald" is going to fight them "No holds barred tooth and nails win lose or draw". The liberal news media steam rolled over the last three republican presidential losers without even having to break a sweat, but not so with Mr. Trump, he is going to take it to the mat.

As a writer of great wisdom one thing I have learned is persistence and determination alone are omnipotent, and I think most super achievers knows this.

Due to our welfare state far too many dependent minded people confuses almost any demand for self-responsibility and self-accountability as racism.
SIRMANS LOG: 15 JUNE 2016, 1003 HOURS.

CAN THE USA SURVIVE ITS INSANITY?
I, as a writer of almost supernatural wisdom can only present the big picture on this whole insane horrific violence matter. I believe what is allowing all of this insane unreasonable violence the USA and western civilization is facing today is the result of weak societal discipline.

The primary head of this monster is the welfare state that results from economic minimum wage laws that blocks built-in free market place societal discipline. The subheads from this monster is out of control liberalism, the destruction of our nuclear and extended family system, the failure to teach and enforce proper norms and traditions to our young, etc.

We now face an out of control political correction liberalism swamp with moten-gators and every kind of anti-survival monster known to man. All seems to be lost, but there is a savior on a white horse standing ready to ride in and save our way of life by draining this swamp.

One simple act will start the healing process that will save our nation and way of life. That act is to repeal the God forsaken insane arch-evil 1938 socialist minimum wage law. Otherwise, there is no hope; the USA will continue to deteriorate until our phony joke of a free market place economy totally collapses.
SIRMANS LOG: 13 JUNE 2016, 1102 HOURS.

WRITER BELIEVES TRUMP REPRESENTS THE

GREATEST THREAT TO OUT OF CONTROL LIBERALISM SINCE THE "NEW DEAL".

I'm going to say something maybe I shouldn't. I believe the dread and fear of Trump by the Dem's and liberals are so strong that some epic high level back stabbing by the Dem's won't surprise me. I believe the writing is on the wall and all of the liberalism marbles is at stake, here.

I believe the Democratic Party and the liberal press is one and the same and on a mission of one thing, political destroy "The Donald" at all cost. I personally believe that anyone failing to vote against the USA Supreme Court being taken over by liberalism is either a liberal or a fool or both. Duh. There goes our right to bear arms.

It is impossible to have a genuine true free market place economy with a minimum wage law in place. The key to the whole USA problem is: Ronald Wilson Reagan said it years ago, "Government cannot solve our problems government is the problem".

Repeal the poison pill 1938 minimum wage law then a true free market place will kick in and save our freedom and keep millions from starving when this world economy soon collapses. Otherwise, we can kiss the USA goodbye as a free and independent nation, we don't even make a lot of our own military equipment anymore.

SIRMANS LOG: 08 JUNE 2016, 1106 HOURS.

45TH PRESIDENT OF THE UNITED STATES OF AMERICA: DONALD J TRUMP

I've said it before and will say it again, Trump forces one to make an emotional choice, "Love him or leave him". His core followers have chosen to love him and after that he can't do no wrong. The ones that have chosen to leave him goes the full range from tuning him out to outright hate.

In private life when one chooses to leave someone they can't stand, usually "Out of sight out of mind" means it is over and done with. However, with Trump running for president and being on TV so much, "Out of sight out of mind" is not so easily done with. The emotional turbulence one wanted to leave behind is now forced to deal with it coming at them from the TV.

I'm one that believes that emotions affect everyone in some way; it seems to get in the air. To evoke strong emotions I believe is a gift that Trump has, and the effect can't be understood using reasoning. Sure, Trump has the ability evoke strong emotions, but the issues that he is addressing are what truly woo his core supporters.

What now really seems to be coming into focus is Trump actually just might win this whole thing, but it won't be due to just his supporters. If Trump wins it will be because it boils down to two choices. The first choice is the democrats paired with liberalism and the second choice is the republicans paired with conservatism.

Personally I don't believe Trump can accomplish most of what he promises, but if he can save the Supreme Court from a liberal takeover, he got my vote. And I believe that most reasonable men/women of common sense and sound judgment will come to that same conclusion. I believe continuing down this road of liberalism we are on leaves no chance of the USA surviving, nil.

At least with Trump out of control liberalism will be put in check and the Supreme Court saved. Yet, the fact remains after years as a welfare state now most Americans can't recognize a survival threat, physical or moral even if it slapped them upside the head.

I'm no genius or rocket scientist, but I know if liberals get total control of the Supreme Court the second amendment and our right to bear arms is history. After many, many years our welfare state has produced an out of proportion amount of naive shallow minded liberals that can't see past their noses.

I'm not a liberal or conservative I'm a realist. And I assure you there is a 100 percent fact that USA citizens will lose their right to bear arms if liberals take over the Supreme Court, period. After our guns are gone it will be only a matter of time before we lose individual freedom followed by private property rights, period. Liberals can't see this coming but I can my friend.
SIRMANS LOG: 25 MAY 2016, 2259 HOURS.

NEW ADD ON UPDATE CONCERNING USA PRESS: 05 JUNE 2016, 1417 HOURS.
The thing about liberals and those that are shallow and uninformed is usually some form of pain is the only thing that forces them to see the light and become enlighten. The downside is we all are in the same survival boat and when all of our freedom and private property rights are gone, oops, now liberals finally see the light. Duh.

Individual freedom is the rare exception in history

and it can't exist very long unless there is a genuine true free market place economy to maintain discipline. Otherwise, creeping do-good liberalism at some point will force a demand for some form of authoritarian rule just to maintain order and some sanity; the USA is nearing that point.

However, there is one last chance to save the USA and western civilization, the USA must repeal our arch-evil 1938 socialist minimum wage law, period. A minimum wage law blocks the disciplinary power of a free market place economy and allows liberalism to grow unabated out of control.

And another thing: I believe for the most part today's free press is about as useless as tits on a boar hog. Most are shallow and liberal and in many cases distorts the news instead of objectively reporting it.

In no way am I criticizing all members of the USA free press, I still think there must be a free press for freedom to exist.

SIRMANS LOG: 05 JUNE 2016, 1743 HOURS.

PS: Haters and those that are against you will try to make you a liar and perfectionist to dehumanize you. I never fall for it, people don't love you because you are perfect, people love you for being human and not perfect.

**GREAT WRITER SHEDS A TEAR
(READ ABOUT JOBS GOING OVER SEAS JUST BELOW)**
Knowing that my country cannot survive unless our strong nuclear and extended family system is

restored is why I plod on. I know that 95 percent or more of the people who read my views vehemently disagrees and feel that I am mean and uncaring.

Sure, I'm neurotic and no saint, but no one has to tell me how it feels to be beaten down, ridiculed, humiliated, laughed at, rejected, and told that I would never amount to anything. I have experienced it all and more. I almost never speak personally about myself because I feel it is self-serving, so forgive that brief relapse, I carry on.

I learned fairly young that except in rare cases people self-destructs and blames it on others. I learned that if one can genuine love and forgive it is almost impossible for anyone to mentally destroy you. As a rule you will almost never find those that can genuine love and forgive in mental wards, in prisons, and loser on the streets or else where.

Nothing has advanced civilization more than determine individuals with an idea or conviction, and against all odds stayed the course, like this writer, Freddie L Sirmans Sr.
SIRMANS LOG: 24 MAY 2016, 1223 HOURS.

JOBS GOING OVERSEAS:
Blaming other nations for our jobs being driven over seas or out of the USA is one the biggest lies that has ever been told. No problem has ever been solved by blaming others for ones own weakness or lack of discipline. The problem with the USA and has been for a long time is out of control government spending, period. No government can support a welfare state very long, time's up.

Every business must make a profit or go out of business. And the cold hard fact is the USA economy would have collapsed back in the early 1990's unless a way was found to cut expenses, that way was a mad dash to find the cheapest labor.

The cheapest labor couldn't be found here in the USA because able-bodied men were already getting a SSI check or sponging off a mother, daughter, or some other female family member.

I'm age 73 now but when I was a kid my grandmother got a check and I still think that was the greatest thing to ever happen to the elderly. However, a welfare state destroys the nuclear and extended family system and there never has and never will be a society that survives with that being the case, period.

All "Wealth" and I mean with practically no exceptions comes from some form of private business profit and the truth is USA businesses don't produce enough profit to support our welfare state. So, how in the hell can you bring jobs back if a business can't afford all of the local, state, and federal taxes, plus license fees, permits, and countless other government mandates.

Businesses trying to make a profit to survive are why the jobs were driven over seas in the first place. Love me or hate me I am only trying to give you the cold hard reality facts. The only thing that has a chance of bringing jobs back and saving the USA and western civilization is to repeal our insane arch-evil 1938 socialist minimum wage law. And you can take that to the bank.

Socialism: I'm hearing just south of us down in

Venezuela with their experiment in socialism and the ignoring of profit has them eating family pets and standing in line all day for food. I believe if the Dem's keep power and liberalism prevails that is where the USA will be in just a few years.

I believe unless the insane Arch-evil 1938 socialist minimum wage law is somehow repealed the USA cannot remain a free nation. Right now most liberals hate profit and don't think it matters. There is no way to keep order and remain a free people with that prevailing mentality, our mostly liberal free press has failed to educate and keep the people truly informed.

Boo! I'm your boogieman.
SIRMANS LOG: 18 MAY 2016, 2343 HOURS.

WRITER, FREDDIE L SIRMANS, SR. THINKS TRUMP WILL PICK A WOMAN RUNNING MATE
think there is a 90 percent possibility that Trump will choose a woman running mate due to his ease of comfort working with strong women in his past. I constant hear of Trump placing strong women in top position throughout his company.

No one knows including him until he makes the final decision, but the percentage of him picking a woman is almost overwhelming.SIRMANS LOG: 17 **MAY 2016, 1114 HOURS.**

NEW ENTRY: 15 MAY 2016
Any conservative that believes our welfare state beast will allow social programs to be cut with pain and them remain in power is a fool in my view. If republican and conservatives do get a Trifecta in November 2016 they will have one last chance to

save the USA and western civilization.

Plus, they can save the USA and western civilization and keep power at the same time by repealing the Godforsaken insane arch-evil 1938 socialism minimum wage law. Doing that will untie our all powerful free market place economy which will absorb all blame and save the USA and western civilization.

That is the only hope of saving individual freedom in the world today, otherwise liberalism will prevail. Liberalism is going to drive the USA into a dictatorship or some other form of authoritarian rule, period. It is impossible to retain a free society without discipline, responsibility, and accountability which is fast going by the wayside here in the USA.

I am a great writer folks, I believe it but when has anyone ever taken my advice, never.
SIRMANS LOG: 15 MAY 2016, 1630 HOURS.

I think most of you have heard the saying "Being dead right", so who wants that? I think when it come to politics many of today's conservatives are just plain shallow and lacks a true understanding of human nature, period.

Sure, for a conservative to focus on cutting social programs is sensible and the right thing to do thirty years or more ago, but today in 2016 it is just plain shallow, dumb, stupid, and a recipe for getting booted out of power. And it is a waste of time because our welfare state beast will never allow any worthwhile cuts anyway.

This full-blown super welfare state we have today has far too many government dependents for any individual or political party to put a dent in it and remain in power. Sure, this welfare state tolerate conservatives now because conservatives holds the moral high ground, but at the first sign of any real hardship and pain due to social programs cuts all conservatives will be booted I assure you.

This great country was built on conservative values and today's conservatives are right for wanting to do the sensible thing and live within our means, but they are too shallow to realize that our welfare state beast is much too powerful. I repeat it is shallow, dumb, and stupid to think any individual or political party can force responsibility and accountability peacefully on our full blown welfare state beast, it Ain't gonna happen.

This is where my almost supernatural wisdom comes into play and I will explain. When speaking of force almost everyone will think in terms of physical force, which is out of the question. The reason a genuine true free market place economy is so successful and will produce far more production than any other system known to man is because of its discipline.

Discipline is the same key ingredient found in every successful system. Nature itself operates on its own law of free "Natural selection". All great nations fall from within and nothing on earth is capable of taking down our welfare state beast, except a true genuine free market place economy, period. Our USA today no longer even comes close to having a true free market place economy.

If conservatives expect to save our USA they have one chance and one shot before being booted out of power, otherwise it is political suicide to expect to take down our welfare state beast and survive in power.

The only way to save the USA and western civilization is to untie the USA economy by repealing the 1938 minimum wage law then a true free market economy will kick in and save our civilization, nothing else has the power to save us. Repealing the 1938 minimum wage law will drain the liberal swamp, boom the economy, and then new growth will abound unhindered, otherwise we will just continue on our path to sure doom. **SIRMANS LOG: 12 MAY 2016, 1749 HOURS.**

SELF-RIGHTEOUSNESS GONE AMUCK

Priorities, priorities, priorities, we here in the USA are fast on our way of not having a country, yet some in high places has their priorities upside down. My great beloved homeland is being ripped to threads by liberalism and ignorance, but without a doubt my first priority is to do what I can to help rein in liberalism.

I may be on the losing side and never get to taste the reward of high achievement, but in defeat my soul will rest knowing I never gave comfort to out-of-control liberalism. Liberalism in itself is not a bad thing; in fact liberalism can be a good thing and make the world a far safer and better place for us all.

However, like food, sex, or anything out-of control, out-of-control liberalism is going to kill us, period. Repealing the insane arch-evil 1938 socialist minimum wage law will re-balance and bring liberalism back under control that is the only thing that can possibly save the USA and western civilization.

SIRMANS LOG: 09 MAY 2016, 1633 HOURS.

**BEGGARS CAN'T BE CHOOSY
NO TRUE CONSERVATIVE WILL CUT OFF HIS
NOSE TO SPITE HIS FACE OR CUT THE BABY
IN HALF, GOOD RIDDANCE.**

**REMEMBER, IT IS THE COUNTRY A TRUE
CONSERVATIVE LOVE AND WANT TO SAVE,
NOT EGOS, AND CERTAINLY NOT ABOUT
HELPING PUT FIVE LIBERALS ON THE
SUPREME COURT. DUH?**

When you are $20,000,000,000,000 in debt as far as I'm concern you are a beggar like it or not. Let me say up front voting for Mr. Trump was not my first choice but I feel I would be a fool not to in the future. I would never help put five liberals on the Supreme Court. However, I'm a writer folks and I write what I truly believe.

Before our welfare state and insane arch-evil 1938 socialist minimum wage law the USA could talk tough and really back it up. Back then the citizens was independent and almost no one was dependent on the government for hardly anything. Now, lets fast forward to the year of 2016, we are a full blown top heavy welfare state with millions upon millions solely dependent on government for survival.

Admit it or not the USA is totally interdependent and need others to survive as much as they need us. In fact all of these liberal induced government dependents have to be fed there is no stable traditional nuclear and extended family safety umbrella to fall back under, the welfare state has destroyed that. Even if no one else has the wisdom to see it, I know the only thing that can save the USA and western civilization is to ban all minimum wage laws. That is the only thing that can rein in liberalism and save us. Banning all minimum wages laws will restore the inner fabric of our nation and wean the overwhelming masses off of the government titty.

The days of the welfare state is over because all wealth comes from some form of private business profit and liberalism is destroying that more and more every day. What the USA have now is a wobbly kneed top-heavy p…. of an economy that is here today but could be gone tomorrow. Yet, liberalism is hammering the final nails in our coffin while my wisdom is totally ignored. Lord have mercy.
SIRMANS LOG: 05 MAY 2016, 1740 HOURS.

WEIRD:
NEW ENTRY: 01 MAY 2016, 1403 HOURS.
Saving the USA and western civilization is simple; just ban all minimum wags laws. Minimum wage laws fuels inflation and inflation fuels welfare states all to the detriment of long term human survival.

The USA and western civilization can't be saved until the old tried and true norms and traditions are first restored, and no amount of money and good jobs alone will do that. Unless all minimum wages laws are banned to rein in liberalism nothing can save the USA.

If your culture and morals are almost totally corrupted more wealth only acts as an enabler to create bigger problems.
SIRMANS LOG: 01 MAY 2016, 1439 HOURS.

Sometimes it seems like I'm the only one with the wisdom to see that the minimum wage law is what gives government almost total power over the private sector. Before the insane arch-evil 1938 socialist minimum wage law was enacted each individual business decided what wages and prices to operate on and unrestricted competition purged out all inflation.

The minimum wage law is what gave the liberals the power to create our welfare state beast back in 1938 by inflating our currency to no end. And ever since that day our culture, morals, and almost everything else has gone to hell in a hand basket. **SIRMANS LOG: 29 APRIL 2016, 1234HOURS.**

All great civilizations falls from within, here in the USA I see it coming every day. The problem with the fallacy of masses of people jumping on a wishful thinking bandwagon is it's like expecting a pot of gold at the end of a rainbow.

The thing about a welfare state is it destroys discipline to the point that very few has a clue as to what raw bare boned survive is all about, I'm seen as a nut case but in survival terms nothing could be further from the truth.

There never has and never will be a nation or society that survived without a stable nuclear and extended family system, period. I hate to say this and hope I'm wrong on this, but I feel western civilization with it's welfare states no longer has the societal discipline, raw wisdom, or the will to survive a full scale economic collapse.

Only banning all minimum wage laws can force the necessary societal discipline on us to prevent our total self-destruction. Liberals and liberalism with its creation of our welfare state is what got us in this dire fix. Its insane to think a liberal parading in conservatives clothing will save us, it ain't gonna happen, yet snake oil is being bought right now on a mass scale.

First things first, nothing can save the USA unless we get back to the basics and reestablish a strong nuclear and extended family system again, banning all minimum wage laws will do just that.

Today most people has forgotten or don't know the basic foundation and building blocks necessary for human society to survive long term, I will give you a brief crude walk through. The number one foundation building block is the nuclear and extended family system and ours are in almost total ruins.

Another foundation building block is to safeguard our small farmers and home gardeners for emergency backup bartering capacity in case our economy collapses, if the economy collapsed today almost no one would have anything to eat or to barter with. And above all the welfare state has blocked strong males from passing on proper norms, traditions, and morals that in the past safeguarded future generations.

Only by banning all minimum wage laws can the necessary societal discipline be forced upon us to save us from ourselves. I am a lone writer with no connections or source of inside information.

In private I'm sure the liberal news media and the Dem's are gloating and patting themselves on the back. Sure, they tolerate Mr. Trump now because they are so convinced that he will lose to Mrs. Clinton.

However, once the general election begins the liberal news media will show no mercy in trying to destroying this great honorable businessman that truly means well. They will leave no stone un-turned looking for muck of every kind. You mark my word. Will they fail, no one knows, we'll see? **SIRMANS LOG: 26 APRIL 2016, 2323 HOURS.**

FINAL SOLUTION TO THE RACE AND ECONOMIC PROBLEM IN THE USA AS SEEN BY GREAT WRITER FREDDIE L SIRMANS SR., A MUST READ.

UPDATED VERSION: AFRICAN AMERICAN EXCUSES, EXCUSES, EXCUSES, AND I'M SICK AND TIRED OF IT. WRITER ATTACKS BLACK LEADERSHIP.

Halt, stop, or brace yourself, because this great writer is fixing to let her rip, go on a tirade, rant, or what ever you may call it. OK, lets just dispense with any bull s... and just talk plain turkey. Sure, there is a lot of racism in America, always has been and always will be. Hell, I may be called a racist, but I think not.

Life is not perfect and this nation is not perfect, but it is the greatest country to ever exist in my view. I love this great country and it is the only home that I have ever known. This great country offers the most individual freedom and opportunity to ever exist on earth, and it still does in spite of our beloved tax and spends liberals, but still I love-um like a brother.

Now, as to my beloved African American race, the problem with us is too much pampering, period. Hell, I'm a neurotic mentally handicapped cripple from my childhood bed wetting days, yet I will never stoop to being just a plain excuse maker. If one accepts excuses for failure an excuse can always be found.

Sure, there may be be a good reason for an excuse, but as for my self I don't want to hear it, I only accept results. Like a coach once said: "you show me a good loser, and I'll show you a loser." I have been counted out all of my life. For me, I have always taken responsibility for my own survival and I know beyond a shadow of doubt that otherwise I wouldn't be standing today.

Today all I hear from African American leadership is what we lack, what we don't have, we don't have jobs, and on and on. However, the question that needs to be asked is: What do we need to do for our community our selves? Duh! And they will all look at each other like helpless sheep. Number one should be how could we provide more of our own jobs in our communities.

We African Americans have our racial priorities mixed up or maybe even misplaced in my view. Everyone's priority should be immediately family first, then community, city, state, country, but ones race can never be totally ignored to fit somewhere in that order.

One must have a mental identity to know who he/she

really is as a person; otherwise one could end up with no true racial identity. Something of the sort has happened to the African American race on a mass scale.

We African Americans as a race mentally see ourselves as dependent like siblings that can't do for ourselves and must be taken care of by the master. And like most siblings we are jealous and compete against each other for the master's favors. That is why you see the herd mentality and we always vote anywhere from 90 percent to 99 percent for one party in almost every election.

We as a race are locked into this dependent sibling psyche. It is not a bad thing, it kept the African American race alive in an almost totally hostile environment right out of slavery. However, circumstance and the nation has evolved and that type of psyche is no longer needed for the black race to survive. Yet, the welfare state won't let blacks escape its dependent mentality.

The only thing that can break this dependency chain is for African Americans to be forced to stand on its own two feet. Folks, I don't have anything to do with reality, I am only telling things as I see them, you have the freedom to totally disagree with anything I write and brand me a fool and idiot, so be it.

The African American race in America is awesome; we hold many of the most powerful elected offices in this great nation, from the office of president on down.

There is no logical reason why African Americans can't employ at least a quarter of the jobs in its own communities, yet I doubt its over 3 percent.

For God sake, grow up African Americans, grab the bull by the horns, and learn to love all people and especially those that look like you. Now, don't you go telling me you don't have hate and contempt for those that look like you? Otherwise, why else would there be all of this mass killings in black communities?

Plus, where you spend your money proves where your first loyalty priority lies and it's certainly not with the man in the mirror. No one is expected to support a dirty greasy spoon eatery, but remember Auburn Avenue and the likes in other cities could equal the best before the welfare state came about. Now, our elites run as far as affordable away from an all black neighborhood and it is all because of our welfare state.

The welfare state has reduced the once proud Negro race to a bunch of government dependent siblings that are constantly at each others throat. We don't trust each other or truly respect each other and is ashamed of an all black neighborhood. And don't give me this bull excuse about high crime, the movie "Raising in the sun" proves blacks couldn't wait to get out long before crime was a problem.

If you don't love who you really are how can you expect other races to respect you. Liberalism is responsible for this sad condition and to this day still patronizes African Americans and hates nothing more than a black that wants to be self sufficient and independent. A black conservative threatens liberals ability to keep African Americans dependent minded and self-rejecting more than anything else.

You black man, you don't truly love your own people, you mentally see yourself like your master and better than that sassy nigger that is undeserving of respect. Besides, you see that sassy nigger as a competitor against you, why should you kiss his ass and help him to get ahead, f... him, I'll spend my money where I want too, and anyone that's got a problem with that can kiss my black ass. This is the type of thinking that goes on in the minds of so many in the African American community.

The only thing that can break this locked-in African American dependency mentality is to kick the young eagle out of the welfare state nest, then it will be forced to fly on its own, that is what the mother eagle does. What I just said is not cold and uncaring, that is being prepared to survive on ones own, and not disappear off this earth when this welfare state soon crashes.

The African American sad condition is the tip of the USA survival spear, or the canary in our culture mine. God save my beloved homeland. Hallelujah.

OK, OK, having aired it out and said my peace, what is the real solution to the African American problem? Anyone familiar with my work should know my constant drum beat for the only thing that can save all of America and even western civilization.

It is the economy, fool! Nothing on earth is more powerful than a genuine true free market place economy; it trumps the law and everything in terms of having and maintaining an orderly society.

However, the USA liberal socialist destroyed our true free market place economy almost eighty years ago by enacting the evil 1938 socialist minimum wage law. And the inner fabric of moral decay and culture rot along with a lack of any emergency bartering capacity has grown unabated ever since.

A true free market place economy must be absolutely free to have the power to discipline itself and the nation, the same as Mother Nature, with its supreme law of natural selection. There must be a survival need for anything in nature to exist, otherwise it starts ceasing to exist based on nature's supreme law of "Natural selection."

The enacting of the 1938 minimum wage law gave the USA government for the first time absolute power over private property rights and business production and distribution. That act for the first time allowed liberals to seize almost absolute power by operating a candy store and promising the moon and back.

Before the 1938 minimum wage law it was almost impossible to inflate the USA currency because the economy had the discipline power to purge out inflation, waste, inefficiency and the likes. Now, the minimum wage law acts as a purge inhibitor and every imaginable negative anti-survival special interest group in America have grown like wild flowers unabated ever since. Mass killing's in the womb and same sex marriages are just new additions to the anti-survival paths the USA is going down.

Negative anti-survival special interest is now a swamp with the coalition power to take down this great nation. Creating our minimum wage law purge inhibitor is like trying to stop nature's life and death cycle, insane. The evil 1938 socialist minimum wage law have an almost over-powering appeal to the economically ignorant, and has all but destroyed our culture, good morals, and any capacity to barter.

A nation can't have emergency bartering capacity without enough small farmers and home gardeners, which is what got the USA through the great depression. I could go on and on with the destruction this evil 1938 socialist minimum wage law has done to this great nation.

But, I will wrap it up by saying this: Everybody and his brother has an opinion, but it is my God given destiny to let you know until the 1938 minimum wage law is repealed it is impossible for the USA to be saved. The "Final solution" is to repeal this evil law, or we perish, period.

I believe all to no avail the federal reserve and politicians trying to save this welfare state beast will eventually sell the nations sovereignty, land, wealth, and mineral rights off like a hooker on the block. Plus, there is no telling what has already been sold off being $18,000,000,000,000 in debt already.

Only a handful of people know, but I seriously doubt there is any gold left at Fort Knox anymore. I can't make anybody believe me; still I believe I understand the workings of an economy as well as anyone. And I promise you this weak phony P.... of an economy the USA have today is almost as useless as tits on a boar hog in terms of saving itself or this great nation.

Repeal the 1938 minimum wage law and give the USA economy back its original power, please Sir/Madam. It is not about how much increase in wages that really count, it is about having a job to buy enough food and necessities to survive at all. What good is a higher wage if you can't afford hardy anything, duh? It won't happen overnight, but repealing the minimum wage law will wean inflation out of our currency so $1.00 will buy what $20.00 will today.

Folks, I don't have to be right on my assessment, and I even hope I'm proven wrong. Why oh Lord, why have I been blessed with so much raw wisdom, it is like a curse, I see things so clearly, why me o-lord. Writer answers that himself: Why not you. Amen.
SIRMANS LOG: 07 MAY 2015, 1328 HOURS.

OBEDIENCE OF THE LAW MUST BE THE FIRST PRIORITY, FAILURE TO DO SO LEAVES NO EXCUSE FOR WHATEVER MAY HAPPEN

We all care about our loved ones. But, the only thing that keeps us from behaving like wild animals in the jungle is the law. The law must be above all else and the top priority for the USA to remain a civilized nation.

The law must be respected and obeyed, period. We now have the law flaunted and disrespected in high places, and after years of our liberal entitlement welfare state many have succumbed to raw subjective emotionalism. Whatever happened to the words "No one is above the law," are they still valid?

You may want to be weak and stupid and live by the rules of the jungle with little or no respect for the law then have at it, just don't include me. I believe in "First things first," period. The law is what protects us all, especially the poor and disadvantage.

Part of what's wrong with this entitlement welfare state now is we have turned into a P.... society with less and less accountability. And it's going to be our downfall, you mark my word. Anyone that succumbs to the weakness of subjective emotionalism is a fool and loser, and is either ignorant or not dealing with a full deck in my view.

If one doesn't love and support unconditional one's own race he is without a true identity and can't really be trusted. It's a fact we African Americans are without a true identity and is searching for love in all of the wrong places. I've heard the chant, black and proud and all of that, but in my view it is just words and lack substance.

We need to believe we as African Americans are as good as any race and need to take pride in behaving and obeying the law as well as any race. If you want to be treated with respect, then act like one deserving respect. I believe we as a race can behave and obey the law as well as any race, and we as a race did too before our liberal entitlement welfare state came about.

SCROLL DOWN TO READ LATEST INJECTION: WE AFRICAN AMERICANS HAS A PRIMITIVE HERD MENTALITY WITH VERY LITTLE FREE INDEPENDENT ACCOUNTABILITY THINKING AMONG US

Most African Americans have a bond to the democrat party like a child to its mother. And no amount of reasoning or logic can break that bond unless the child becomes a free independent minded thinker. Natures law of "taking the course of least resistance" dictates that almost no one is going to become a free independent accountability thinker unless forced to.

The herd won't allow free independent accountability thinking within the herd itself and even when an individual does it anyway he is branded a traitor or nut case. Hell, I love my country the only home I know and I feel if you are wrong you deserve to be called out even if you are a sister, brother, or mother.

I don't believe in pampering anyone, you are responsible for your own actions. To err is human, and forgiveness is the foundation of the Christian religion in my view. I'm one that believes that civilization would never have gotten out of the Dark Age without the Christian religion and its power of forgiveness.

My God, I watch the local news almost everyday and

its smash and grab, armed robbery, breaking and interring, muggings, and crime galore. And guess who is doing almost all of this crime? You fill in the blank. Yet, all I hear from white liberals and black liberals is patronizing and misplaced guilt and no accountability what so ever, it's insane.

Before the "New deal" a trip behind the shed or woodpile would always keep the would be future criminals on the straight and narrow good citizen course and out of prison. Since that's not done very much any more the best thing that would do the most good for young future black criminals would be medical supervised flogging.

Four or five hard lick on the ass would do far more good than 5-10 in the pen and it wouldn't cost the tax payers. That would put a stop to this paying to produce a more harden and cunning criminal. But, that will never happen, oh, no, we are too civilized for that, yet, the cancer of crime is splitting this great country into racial camps, duh.

Only one thing can save the great USA now: repeal the cruel evil 1938 socialist minimum wage law, then there will be no government forced wage control. That would get rid of any forced wage control entirely. That is the only way this great nation can be saved from itself, period. Repeal it now tomorrow may be too late.
SIRMANS LOG: 30 NOVEMBER 2014, 2123 HOURS

INJECTION: 02 DECEMBER 2014, 1232 HOURS
A huge disadvantage with African Americans having a

herd mentality is it has allows a very few poverty pimps to exploit and keep alive this still-a-victim big, big, big, lie. And as long as we have our liberal induced welfare state I see very little chance of African Americans ever being forced to take responsibility and stand on their own to gain a do-and-think-for -yourself mentality.

Sure, I may be hated for my views now, but there will come a day when I will be loved for my great wisdom and foresight, glory be to God.

Just look at our African American situation, in some neighborhoods there is not a husband to be found for miles. And even if you can find a man living in some of the homes all he is there for is companionship and stud service at her whim. Uncle Sam is the real sugar daddy, a poor man can't compete. Come on y'all give me a break now, instead of all of this rioting we as a race ought to be cleaning up our own house.

We ought to be instilling in our young discipline and self-respect and respect for other people and their property, too. Shame on us for not knowing how to behave and obey the law like other races does. Other races have eyes; they see who is committing all of these crimes. Reality is reality, don't insult my intelligence.

Sure, we as race are guilty of keeping a child's mentality including a fierce sibling rivalry against those who look like us. That is why African Americans can't advance as a race; we won't readily support each other in business or otherwise unless there is no other good choice. And even our elites will try to get as far away from an all black neighborhood as they can afford.

All other races create different pecking order level surrounding zones in their own race's community, lets face facts, and it takes an independent minded adult to escape childhood sibling rivalry. And the first thing it takes to do that is the ability to forgive all people. Otherwise, un-forgiveness locks one in to that situation, then if one is still hating and un-forgiving seventy years later they will still have that fierce dependent minded sibling rivalry from childhood.

To escape here is a simple formula to repeat to yourself over and over until you mean it: "I can wish all people goodwill (through God who strengthens me), optional if you are a Christian." That will free one to become an independent thinker.

I never intended to get sidetracked off into all of this theory stuff, it seems as if my pen took on a life of its own, sorry. Sure, we as a race have some guilt in my view, but again the real arch villain behind the scene is the heavy hand of our liberal induced welfare state beast pulling the strings.

However, before the new deal African Americans had almost thrown off their dependency minded slave mentality, but the welfare state nipped all of that in the bud. Before the new deal blacks supported each other, and we had poor, middle class, and upper class zones in the same community. Plus, we had far more black owned businesses than today. Every town had a booming chitlin's circuit and great entertainment.

We were about to become of age. But, the New deal kicked the poor black man out of the house. After that no one instilled discipline, proper norms, and traditions in our young and we lost our way. After all of that our dependency minded slave mentality returned with a vengeance and the democrat party and the welfare state is now our new slave masters.

SIRMANS LOG: 02 DECEMBER 2014, 1232 HOURS

FERGUSON IS A WAKE-UP CALL ON WHAT CULTURE ROT AND MORAL DECAY HAS DONE TO THE USA DUE TO OUR LIBERAL INDUCED WELFARE STATE
NEW INJECTION #2, 25 NOVEMBER 2014, 1907 HOURS

What we African Americans need to realize is each of us is an ambassador for our race. Many years ago we blacks knew that, but that seems to be lost now a days. A good or bad stereotype image affects all of us in some way, you can't escape it.

Call it what you may but there is no denying the fact that African Americans are committing far more crimes than any race on earth proportional-wise. The main reason for that is lack of parents instilling self-restraint and self-accountability in their young. A lack of self-restraint and self-accountability breeds disrespect for authority and the rights of others.

That is what's driving this out of control cancer in the African American community call crime. But, the actual real villain driving everything from behind the curtain is our liberal induced welfare state beast, with the ability to throw a rock and hide its hand. I stand by my prediction that the USA economy will collapse in 2015 unless our cruel evil 1938 socialist minimum wage law is repealed.

I see all of the economically ignorant do-gooders believing that raising the minimum wage will help people, but, in reality it will only speed up our pace to an economy collapsing doom. Getting rid of any wage or price control entirely is our only way out, because that will restore power back to the people then the people will need very little money and live off the land if need to.

However, there has never been a case of government changing course knowing it is headed to doom, it is not in its DNA. The powers that be is going to feed this tax hungry gobbling welfare state beast to the last crumb.

They will never stop feeding the beast and I will never stop drum beating to repeal our evil 1938 socialist minimum wage law to save the only home and way of life I know. Glory be to God.

SIRMANS LOG: 25 NOVEMBER 2014, 1907 HOURS

NEW INJECTION: 24 NOVEMBER 2014, 0853 HOURS

Never in the history of mankind has the poor ever been liberal and moral corrupted until the "New deal" programs created a baby welfare state around 81 years ago. Now we have more poor killing babies in the womb and neutralizing their seed in other ways than any demographic group. No hardship or struggle breeds liberalism and a weak survival instinct.

Anyone with a strong survival instinct (like me) will instinctly know the unborn must be protected for the long term survival of the species. The fact is the USA simply cannot and will not survive unless the cruel evil 1938 socialist minimum wage law is repealed. Any and all types of wage or price controls must be removed entirely.

That will set the all powerful free market place free to save the USA and western civilization, too. Look at the immigration problem in the USA and around the world, its going to engulf us, there is no human solution.

However, if the USA free market was set free by repealing the evil 1938 socialist minimum wage law, then a genuine true free market place armed with nature's supreme law of natural selection would solve the problem and save the USA and western civilization, too.

SIRMANS LOG: 24 NOVEMBER 2014, 0853 HOURS
PS: I believe they are really fixing to financially knife and gut our beloved military like never before.

WE AFRICAN AMERICANS ARE NOW TREATED LIKE A BUCK TOOTH REDHEADED STEP CHILD BY THE DEMS

Political speaking African Americans are now the redheaded step child of the Democrat party. This child has a dependency slave mentality and is totally loyal to his/her care taker. Yet, this child's dependency and loyalty is taken for granted. And now a new adoptee is being favored and groomed ahead of this child, sad, sad.

This child loves and wants to be just like his care taker in every way. This dependent child sees the complexion of his care taker and feels that represents the ideal way one need to be.

However, when the child looks in the mirror he doesn't look like his care taker physically but mentally wants to be as much like his care taker as possible. Plus, this dependent child sees others that look like him as competitors, or even the enemy in winning the most favorite one's role by his care taker. That is why African Americans won't readily support each other in businesses or otherwise if there is a choice. And the beat continues on, as long as this child retains his slave dependency mentality he will not escape his predicament, ever.

The only way out and for this child to acquire free objective independent thinking is to shed his dependent slave mentality. That is a lot easier said than done. It is much easier to follow the herd than to veer off into the unknown and entirely fend for yourself. Also, to take that giant step it is almost impossible when there is a welfare state promising to take care of all in need from cradle to grave.

To take the course of least resistance is embedded in us all. The only thing that is going to get African Americans to be free thinker and independent minded is for the crutch to be kicked from under us. To hell with the victimized mentality, its time African Americans take responsibility individually and as a race and feel responsible for their own survival.

Its time we pull up our pants and face down bad behavior, we know right from wrong, enough of this kindergarten blame, blame, blame game. This cancer crime is out of control in our race and we act like its someone else's problem. There was a time when we blacks had self-respect and behaved as well as any race of people. Why should the Dems treat us with respect, they will continually throwing us a bone every now and then and keep treating us like a buck tooth redheaded step child.

If not for this sinister welfare state African Americans would have long ago shed our dependency slave mentality and still have mostly two parent families.
SIRMANS LOG: 22 NOVEMBER 2014, 1406 HOURS

GREAT WRITER FREDDIE L SIRMANS SR GIVES THE ROCK-HARD COLD-STEEL TRUTH ON DOMESTIC ABUSE

All I hear is abuse, abuse, wife abuse, child abuse, women abuse and on and on to no end. Liberal women are almost up in arms; and if it was left up to them they would de-nut all men and make sissies out of all of us. To me there is no mystery here, men are just being men, and it is just cause and effect in action in my view. Men are aggressive creatures by nature and are only doing what they are allowed to get away with. And it is a pipe dream to expect law enforcement to do more than put a dent in it.

It takes fighting fire with fire to really stamp out or completely get under control domestic type violence of this sort. It takes a lot of loved ones that are willing to make a personal sacrifice to truly stamp out or control domestic violence. There has always been some domestic abuse but never out of control like what we are seeing today.

What we are seeing today is the result of a lack of the

strong nuclear and extended family unit. Today we have too few no-none-sense kick-ass dads or brothers that are prepared to go to hell or prison before they will tolerate this sort of abuse on a love one. We are too busy using the "N" word on each other to give a damn. Very few cousins or good friends are prepared to make such a sacrifice.

I have personally heard a few men say that the only thing keeping me off her ass is her dad would kill me. Sure, law enforcement will do their job and enforce the law, but no law enforcement agency can protect private citizens 24-7 day in and day out. Even if women are the weaker sex old man colt solved that imbalance many, many years ago by creating an equalizer. But, the thing about that is not all of us have the will or the guts to send a S.O.B. to hell.
SIRMANS LOG: 19 SEPTEMBER 2014, 2216 HOURS

It really is a waste of time trying to get a liberal to understand freedom and a free market place. That is why most of the world is poor and will always be poor. The point I'm making is liberals don't really understand freedom. Freedom means every individual has a free choice. Jobs don't just drop out of heaven, someone just like you and I must create or provide a job.

This is the land of the free and no one puts a gun to anyone's head and forces them to work for minimum wages. Everyone in this great country has the right to create his/her own job or quit any job one doesn't like. Most liberals think it is wrong for some people to enjoy the rich life while most stay poor. Right now if the liberals had the power they would take almost everything from the rich and spend it on social programs.

They are too shallow minded to realize that rich people

are not stupid. They really believe rich people would continue producing and providing jobs while almost all of their earnings are being taken away. I just can't understand how anyone with any common sense could be so shallow, but they are, and are running the country, too.

There never has and never will be a rich and wealthy nation without a lot of rich greedy people to make it happen. If left entirely up to the liberals the USA would in no time be a third world nation. Yet, enough wanting something for nothing voters keep the tax and spend liberals in power while the country goes to hell in a hand basket.

SIRMANS LOG: 12 JANUARY 2014, 2341 HOURS

A HALF OF A LOAF IS BETTER THAN NOTHING! IF YOU THINK IT'S GETTING BAD NOW WITH OBAMACARE, YOU HAVEN'T SEEN NOTHING YET, YOU JUST WAIT, IF THE DEM'S WIN ANYTHING IN NOV. 2014, THEN WE WILL GET THE FULL THROBBING PURPLE SHAFT FROM THE DEMOCRATS. THEY WANT TO FIRST SECURE THE 2014 MIDTERM ELECTION BEFORE THEY RAM THE FULL SHAFT TO US. IT WILL BE EVEN LESS JOBS AND A TRILLION MORE IN DEBT. IT WILL BE LIKE DETROIT CITY NATIONWIDE! THINK ABOUT IT, WE WILL THEN GET ALL OF OBAMACARE, AND DRY, TOO. GOD, I ASK IN YOUR NAME SAVE THIS GREAT NATION.

It doesn't bother me a lot when I don't sell a lot of books. That is because I estimate only around 2 percent of the American population has the depth and wisdom to truly understand what the hell I be talking about. So be it, I carry on.

They can't get pass the fact that it is not the amount of money that truly matters; it is the buying power that really counts. Before the New deal which started the welfare state $5.00 would buy more than $50.00 will today.

Repealing the minimum wage law would put the provider role back into the hands of the people and allow this great country to survive. Otherwise, there is no way in hell the USA is going to survive on its present course.

Just keep on believing in this phony minimum wage economy and without a doubt within a year I will be proven right. We'll soon see just how nutty my predictions are.

The repeal of the minimum wage law is our savior, but, 98 percent of the population can't get pass believing more and bigger is always better. But, to me a half of a loaf is better than nothing because nothing is what this nation is going to get if we don't change course.
SIRMANS LOG: 29 DECEMBER 2013, 1022 HOURS

MAN/WOMAN OVERBOARD, USA ECONOMY SHIP IS BEGINNING TO SINK!
Folks, I'm just a lowly unknown writer out here pounding away trying to get through to thick sculls. Very few actually know about me or my books, and most of those that do are not interesting in tough

accountability and responsibility. But, I know without a doubt at some point my writing will be vindicated.

Reality is reality there is just no way of getting around that fact. Sure, sometimes it takes a while for the results to catch up but there are no free rides in life someone always pays. The liberals and Dem's have been very successful; they have created masses upon masses of government dependents. They have convinced these dependents that government will always be there to take care of them and their needs.

That is not reality that is the biggest lie that has ever been told. There has never been a government that didn't go broke at some point. The free market place made the USA the most richest and powerful nation to ever exist. The government didn't do that, the free market place did that. Now, I believe most of the people running our government today doesn't even believe in a free market place.

I believe most of the people in charge of our government today are socialist or communist at heart. Everyone seems to be so surprised about how the liberals and Dem's connived and forced Obamacare down our throats. There is nothing new here about liberals in my view. How in the hell do you think the liberals and Dem's held on to the USA house of Representative for 40 consecutive years.

They did it by lying and conniving, and that is what is really happening with this Obamacare website. They will never let it work right before the November 2014 election. They intend to keep the confusion going and never let all of the high costs be widely known before the 2014 election. But, God help us if the Dem's win anything in November 2014, because if they do they are going to ram the full purple shaft to this free nation, e.g. Obamacare dry like it or not.

I believe these people are hardcore ideologues and will go down with the ship before yielding an inch, and believe me that is exactly what is about to happen. Trust me, this USA economy ship is taking on too big of a load and is beginning to sink. This ship is going down unless most of its government load is jettisoned, and fast.

However, the only way to lighten governments load is to kick it out of its social and family provider role. And the way to do that is repeal the minimum wage law or else, this economy ship is going down. I suspect many of the rats have already left the ship in spirit and have property in in places like New Zealand and Australia.
SIRMANS LOG: 26 DECEMBER 2013, 1840 HOURS

WHO IS THE AFRICAN AMERICAN COMMUNITY'S DADDY?
I'm fixing to briefly weigh in on something I have no business touching, besides, some people think of me as a nut case anyway. What if I am off the beaten path that don't mean my beliefs are wrong. Even a broken clock is right twice a day. Concerning two great black

athletes that is at loggerheads: Long before O. J. got into trouble, guess who was always on his case for being too white? Go figure? Some people just naturally goes against the grain, enough said. The problem with the African American race as a whole is culture.

The welfare state has destroyed the African American family structure and community. But, that don't mean we have to take it lying down and still not feel responsible for our own behavior and survival. I don't have the power to stop anything, but you can bet your bottom dollar that I will never make excuses for bad behavior. And no matter who does it I'm not accepting any excuses because of what happened in the distance past.

Grow up African Americans and take responsibility for the behavior of yourself and that of your race. This welfare state has destroyed accountability and responsibility throughout all of America and I'm sick and tired of it. Today a decent law abiding black man can't walk into many stores without being feared because we as a race won't clean up our own community house.

Don't tell me that ain't from a lack of feeling responsible for our own behavior as individuals and as a race. We still have a dependent slave mentality and think it's the white mans fault. The only cure for that is for someone to kick the crutch from under us and demand we stand on our own two feet. Independent minded people don't look to blame and find excuses to fail. I know I may sounds cold, but this USA economy is fixing to collapse and we black folks need to wake up and be prepared, now.

Every preacher in the pulpit and any member in the black community with an ounce of authority need to feel responsible for this cancer in our community called crime. I don't mean taking any physical action we have law enforcement for that. What I'm talking about is taking a moral stand instead of not feeling racially responsible for bad behavior in our youth.

If we don't save our youths no other race will. I didn't intend to vent like this, I just got carried away but something's need to be said. The so called African American leadership is out to lunch.

SIRMANS LOG: 18 DECEMBER 2013, 1750 HOURS

THERE IS NO GOVERNMENT SYSTEM EVER TO EXIST MORE SELF-DESTRUCTIVE THAN A WELFARE STATE!

Like a junkie on the streets trying to get a fix there is nothing a welfare state won't sell off to support its seized social and family provider role. As long as the USA government stays in its social and family provider role it will be impossible for the USA to stop reckless spending or survive.

Right now, the liberals doesn't have the survival instinct or the wisdom to see a real need to stop spending. They are living in the moment and can't see any real danger in reckless spending, and you couple that with an economically ignorant main stream press and general public, all I know to do is pray.

Abolishing the minimum wage law will give the social and family provider role back to the people where it belongs and has always been until the "New deal" seized it in 1938. God I ask in your name, "Save the USA." Time is a winding down, I don't know how much we have left, but, I know beyond a shadow of doubt that a total economic collapse is near unless drastic changes are made.

When I look at the future I think the republicans will soon get the power to have their shot at this health care thing. But, I have news for them too, just like the Dem's they think government can keep and hold on to its social and family provider role, wrong.

I believe unless the republicans and conservatives set about abolishing the minimum wage law they will be seen as phony liberals and quickly replaced. But, of course do like the Dem's never admit in advance what your real intentions are, just git in there and rid the country of this Minimum wage law. It's a free market place killer. See Sirmans survival plan further down.

Most of the big cities water, sewage, and bridges infrastructure were built before a minimum wage law, so, don't tell me junking the minimum wage law won't save this great nation. And here is the real kicker: The USA economy is still the economic engine of the world and if it collapses it takes the world economy down with it. Sure, the world economy may bail us, but not before owning us.

The apple cart has been upset and the only thing that can save the USA is a true free market place. Pure communism and socialism never has and never will work, but, now we have a new monster far worse than both of those systems to contend with, it's called the welfare state. There is no system ever to exist more self-destructive than a welfare state.

It leaves almost no survival tools in place to survival on when nature's bust cycle comes around or if the economy collapses. It really is no joke when I say it may be all the way back to the Stone age for modern civilization. We have no strong nuclear and extended family system to survive on. We have centralized factory farming for our meats and vegetables and hardly any small farmers and home gardeners.

That means we have no adequate emergency backup bartering capacity if the economy collapses and money is worthless. And on and on, our family morals and values would make dog eat dog look like a Sunday picnic after a week into a collapse. Wages and prices must be free floating for a genuine free market place to work and that can't happen with a minimum wage law or any kind of wage or price control.

The consumer cost of living is what's going to kill off the USA economy and Obamacare just speeds up the process. Here is the Ultimatum: Either the USA government abolish the minimum wage law which will free the people to save themselves and the country, or it tries to consolidate and hold on to its current social and family provider role.

If it chooses the latter there is no doubt in my mind that it will to no avail sell off the country to foreigners to try to hang on to a role it shouldn't be in, in the first place. You just watch, and the wait won't be very long. I can dissect an economy as well as anyone and that is what I predict is going to happen. You can't get blood out of a turnip.

I doubt there is any gold left at Fort Knox and there is no telling what else has already been sold off by the federal reserve. I'm telling you as a man of great super natural wisdom, unless the minimum wage law is abolished we might as well kiss our freedom and this great country good by forever.

SIRMANS LOG: 04 DECEMBER 2013, 2217 HOURS

AMERICA! YOU HAVE BEEN SOLD A FALSE BILL OF GOODS

There is a sucker born everyday. It amazes me how gullible people are. They have fallen for this cock & bull big lie that the Obamacare website is somehow a big screw-up, wrong. I for one don't buy that for one second. A computer or a website must obey what it is programmed to do.

The problem is: There is no way in the hell liberals and Dem's are going to let it be known on a large scale the double and triple cost the people will face until after November 2014. Get a grip America; you have been sold a false bill of goods. And be prepared for a never ending list of excuses, but, you will never get a proper working website with cost no matter what you are told. I rest my case.

SIRMANS LOG: 30 NOVEMBER 2013, 2216 HOURS

THE FOLLY OF THINKING THE USA BUDGET CAN BE BALANCED???

A genuine true non-phony free market place economy without exception must be able to set its own wages and prices, period. The liberals in charge of the government seized that right when they enacted the evil 1938 socialist minimum wage law.

That act castrated the USA economy and has led to the destruction of our culture and morals. And until the USA economy is given back its power by repealing the evil 1938 socialist minimum wage law nothing can break the liberals choke hold on this great nation. Otherwise, there is simply no way this great nation of individual freedom can ever be saved.

Men and women of sound mind with strong survival instincts must give the USA economy back its true power, that way it can save this great nation. Nothing else has the power and discipline to drain this vast liberal swamp and prevent individual freedom from disappearing off the face of the earth forever. God save the USA the last bastion of true individual freedom left in the world today.

The truth of the matter is government is actually a parasite; it can only survive if it has a host to take from. Government is not part of the economy but what it does greatly affects the economy. Every society must have a means of protecting itself from internal and external threats and dangers, and that makes having some form of government a must.

Most governments have the power to take over that is why most private sector host has strong built in protections and total control over the money supply. But, like they say, "The way to hell is paved with good intentions."

On the surface the government doing good and helping people doesn't seem like a threat, and it is not in perspective on a temporary basis. But, in reality government must never become a social and family provider more than on a temporary basis if a free nation is to survive long term.

Whoever is the provider is the boss like it or not. That is why in the USA and Western Europe for all practical purpose the welfare state has taken over. Today there are far too many people dependent on the government to ever put government spending on a diet.

In Western Europe and now in the USA the money priority first goes to the welfare state over the military and all else. And there is only contempt for the profit driven private business enterprise host. Plus, private business days may be numbers because liberal media and the masses don't understand profit and hate it.

Still, there is a savior waiting on a white horse ready to

ride in to rescue western civilization. But first, the evil 1938 socialist minimum law must be shot with a silver bullet or a stake driven through its heart by repealing or getting rid of all minimum wage laws entirely. This evil poison pill law must be buried to never rise again for any democracy to ever be safe.

In terms of raw bare boned survival using good intentions and doing the right thing may cause Mother Nature to spit in your face. Just look at the animal kingdom with raw nature, there is no place for good intentions or doing the right thing, except to starve.

Now, you look at the USA economic situation, from a political point of view good intentions and doing the right thing I believe will surely get you booted out of power, period. Folks, let me stop right here and explain, I'm a writer and I write it as I see it. I can be wrong, in fact I hope I am wrong on some of the dire things I see coming down the pike.

I have said it before and am going to say it again, anyone that still thinks the USA and western Europe can be saved as welfare states is economically ignorant in my view. Maybe I'm the one who is ignorant. However, I believe I can dissect and understand the inner workings of an economy as well as anyone. Yet, for the life of me I can't see any social and family provider welfare state doing anything but slowly devouring its own survival host, which is private business enterprise. Economically, it is just impossible for a welfare state to survive very much longer by constantly dwindling its own only survival host, which is profit driven private business enterprise.

Government can take only so much profit before there is none left to take. Anyone with common sense should know that the USA can't forever reckless spend and keep going deeper and deeper into debt. A reasonable person should conclude that the right thing to do is balance the budget and get your physical house in order.

Sure, that is the responsible thing to do if you are talking about around 80 years ago right after the minimum wage law was enacted. But, today for a political party to take that type of normal responsible action is political suicide.

Now, here is where my super wisdom comes into play. OK, lets just imagine that at the snap of fingers all of the USA debts are paid free and clear, do you think the health of the nation would be solved? My answer would be no! Our debt is a currency problem but civilization existed long before a currency was invented.
The main problems with the USA and western civilization are culture and moral in my view. Contrary to the common view I believe in free nations the economy is the real disciplinarian that actually guards and protects the nations culture and morals.

Sure, we are a nation ruled by law not by man, but I believe the economy is the real power that pulls the strings behind the scene. Also, I believe liberalism is actually what's destroying the USA, which could never have happen with a genuine true free market place economy.

I feel the economy the USA has today is a phony P.... of an economy and has been that way ever since the evil 1938 minimum wage law was enacted. The economy the USA has today doesn't have the power or discipline to protect itself or the nation's culture and morals.

Once the 1938 minimum wage law was enacted, that allowed liberalism a foot in the door to inflate the currency and grow government to no end. Since then the minimum wage law gave government absolute power over prices and wages. Once that happened the aggressive liberals has played to the basic weaknesses in our human nature by promising the moon and back. The minimum wage law gave government complete control over private property rights and private business enterprise, which it had never had before in the history of the country. By repealing the minimum wage law the economy would regain its power to guard and protect the nations culture and morals, plus boom the economy in real growth not any phony inflated growth like today.

So, the republican think they can take on our welfare state beast and balance the budget, plus remain in power. Well, I'm one that thinks they are in for a very rude awakening. I hope I'm wrong, but I think the beast will defend itself and win. I truly feel only a genuine true free market place economy minus any minimum wage law has the power and ability to take down this beast.

They will never agree with me, but I feel the only wise course the republicans has left to save the USA is to repeal the evil 1938 socialist minimum wage law, "That is all she wrote." As to liberals saving the country, they are the ones hell bent on destroying it and too shallow to even realize it.

SIRMANS LOG: 17 MARCH 2015, 1748 HOURS.

THE END

**Writer's website:
www.FLSirmans.com**